The Quest for the Pearl

A Myth
for the
New Millennium

Jeremy Naydler

Abzu Press
Oxford
2000

The Quest for the Pearl:
a myth for the new millennium
© Jeremy Naydler, 2000
All rights reserved

This booklet is the text of a talk given for the
Jupiter Trust on October 29th, 1999.

Published and produced by *Abzu Press*
18 Courtfield Road, Oxford OX33 1HA

British Library Cataloguing-in-Publication Data
A catalogue record for this book is
available from the British Library

ISBN 1 898497 37 0

The Quest for the Pearl

Kali Yuga

There is an ancient Hindu tradition that history unfolds in four ages or *yugas*.[1] The first is a long "golden age" (*Krita Yuga)* when people live in harmony with the gods and the cosmos, scarcely aware of the physical dimension. Through succeeding ages (the *Treta Yuga*, the *Devapara Yuga* and finally the *Kali Yuga*) human beings become increasingly distanced from the gods, and become more and more involved in the material world.

According to this tradition, our age is the last of the four ages: the *Kali Yuga* or dark age. It was supposed to have begun shortly before 3000 BC, and lasts for about five thousand years.[2] *Kali Yuga* is characterised by a gradual forgetting of our divine origins, an eclipse of the old awareness of the gods, as human consciousness becomes ever more circumscribed by material conditions. It brings in its wake war, social chaos, famine, and ecological disasters on a massive scale, because human beings come ever more under the influence of the principle of separation: separation not just from the divine world but also from the spirit within nature and within other human beings. *Kali Yuga* is the age of ego-consciousness, when people are very aware of their own separate individuality but find it difficult to relate to that of others.

Another characteristic of *Kali Yuga* is that it is the shortest of the four ages. So time is speeded up, everything happens faster, people live less long (in the *Krita Yuga* the average lifespan was 400 years), time is compressed, space is compressed. This quality of *Kali Yuga* has been referred to by René Guénon as a kind of "solidification" of the world.[3] The world is more and more dense, for it is no longer permeated by spiritual light. People lose their sense of wonder. Even children, to whom wonder comes so naturally,

1

are infected by an increasing cynicism and jadedness in their attitude to life.

Holding Back the Flow of History

This view of history as involving a slow descent from the divine world and a gradual encrustation of the human spirit in matter is not just Hindu. One finds an almost identical teaching in the 8th century Greek poet Hesiod, who talks of a similar decline through a golden age, silver age, bronze age, age of heroes to a final iron age.[4] A very similar perspective existed in many ancient cultures - both the ancient Mesopotamians and the ancient Egyptians had a comparable view, and one also finds something similar in the Persian Zendavesta.[5]

So how did those ancient cultures relate to the historical process? At the beginning of Kali Yuga, the major preoccupation of these ancient societies was to try to hold back the degenerative, downward flow of history. In Egypt, for example, there was the constant attempt to bring the present time into relationship with the "First Time", when humans lived in the lap of the gods.[6] Each coronation of a new king was seen as an opportunity to restore the whole country to harmony with the cosmos again - to restore it to Maat, the cosmic order. Similarly, in the temples, the purpose of the daily temple rituals was to maintain the presence of the gods on earth: there was a huge effort to stem the tide of history that was running away from contact with the divine world.

This is of course a completely different view of history from the prevalent view at the end of Kali Yuga, when people don't talk about the gods, but about their standard of living, about the health service, and about the latest communications technology. At the end of Kali Yuga, it is difficult for people to understand the ancient view of human origins that sees us as

2

having *descended* from a more elevated spiritual state. The orthodox scientific view today is rather that we have *ascended* from a prior apelike condition, struggled up through barbarity to our present condition of civilization. At the end of *Kali Yuga,* we are fixated on the idea of progress, conceived mostly in material terms. The ancient cultures are seen as ignorant and superstitious, and the last thing anyone wants to do is *go back* - and certainly not to some hypothetical paleolithic golden age.

The Hymn of the Pearl

The view of human history as involving a decline or descent from a previous state of spiritual bliss and harmony with the divine has always been the consensus view of most metaphysical and esoteric traditions. We also meet it in many religions, for example in the Biblical myth of the Garden of Eden and the Fall. For those of us who feel there is something more than just superstition or ignorance in such a view, there is a very specific question that arises. The question is: what has been the point of it? And where do we go from here? By way of answering this question, I want to recount a story that originated in ancient Persia, and then became absorbed into the later gnostic tradition. We have it in both a Syriac and a Greek version, and it is known as "The Hymn of the Pearl".[7]

The story tells of a young prince who spends his childhood blissfully happy in the home of his parents, surrounded by an atmosphere of light and love. He wears a beautiful garment made of woven light. But when he grows up, his parents send him away on a mission to "go down" into a foreign country and bring back a pearl which is guarded by a very large and ugly serpent monster that lives in the midst of a bustling city.

3

It is a very long and arduous journey, and in order to embark on it the prince has to take off his garment of light. The way is described as "dangerous and harsh" and one must imagine that many times the prince was tempted to turn back, abandon the journey and return to his parents without the pearl.

At last he arrives in the foreign city, where the serpent resides, and where everyone seems to have fallen under its power. In order not to look like a foreigner and arouse people's suspicions, the prince dresses himself in clothes like theirs, woven of ordinary cloth. He goes to stay at an inn, and in case anyone should suspect him of coming to steal the precious pearl, he mingles with the people, and drinks with them there at the inn. And then he eats their food. And then he falls into a state of profound slumber. He forgets that he is a prince, he forgets that he has a mission. He too falls under the spell of the serpent.

Meanwhile, his parents in the world of light become concerned, and they send an eagle with a message to him to wake up and remember he is a prince, remember that he used to wear a robe woven of light, remember that he has a task to fulfill. When the eagle finds him, asleep at the inn, it rouses him, and the prince does remember who he is and what he is there for. He gets up, summons his courage, and goes to confront the serpent that is coiled around the pearl. Simply by reciting the names of his heavenly mother and father, he is able to overcome the serpent. Then he takes the pearl. He casts off the clothes he has put on and the eagle now guides him back to his homeland. There he puts on his garment of woven light again which has become even brighter and more radiant, because of his victorious travails, and he is received jubilantly by the king and queen to whom he gives the pearl.

The Two Dangers

In this story we see how at the beginning the prince lives in a state of blissful but unconscious union with the Mother/Father God. He then has to be sent down into the foreign land in order that he find *through his own efforts* the pearl of the divine that has become imprisoned within the material world, and return with it to his divine parents. His task can be understood as being to liberate something of the divine nature that has immeasurable value, but lies spellbound within the world.

But we also see that there were dangers involved in this whole enterprise. Two dangers in particular. First of all, there was the danger that the prince, on the outward journey, would find it too hard. Instead of going on down into the foreign land, there was the danger that he would *turn back too soon*. In a sense, this was exactly the temptation of the cultures at the beginning of *Kali Yuga* like ancient Egypt, that sought to slow down or even reverse the journey of descent into materiality. Ancient spirituality was very much geared toward returning to the stars, reuniting with heaven, and this involved the temptation to return before a real separation had occurred.[8] The second danger was that the prince, once having entered the foreign country and having experienced separation from the divine world of his origins, should completely forget his true identity and higher purpose. We could say that the Father/Mother God was taking an enormous risk, a cosmic gamble, in sending the prince out on this mission because they might completely lose their divine child who could be ovepowered by the serpent. And then the precious pearl would remain within the serpent's coils.

In metaphysical or cosmological terms, then, we could say that the relationship between humanity and the divine world is acted out between a polarity of two quite different and potentially - but not necessarily - contrary desires or longings.

On the one hand, there is *the longing to return* to our divine home, return to our divine origins, and this can manifest in a world-rejecting type of spirituality. The danger is that we return too soon or in the wrong way. On the other hand, there is the *drive towards separation* from the spiritual world, to stand in complete independence from any relationship to the spiritual, for only then can we act in freedom. But the danger here is that we separate so completely that we lose all possibility of finding our way back. Ideally, what is needed is the kind of separation that leads to a free and fully conscious return. Only then can the pearl be won.

The Dream of Disincarnation

I have characterised the first tendency, the longing to return, as being especially strong at the beginning of the cycle, in the phase of the the journey of the human spirit away from the divine world, perhaps especially as it enters the age of *Kali Yuga*. It manifests as a great reluctance to engage with the material world, and a longing for our cosmic home in the stars. But in modern times, the impulse is still there, and one can see it erupt in a number of different ways in the world today - none of them particularly healthy and some of them extremely questionable.

In the United States, there are certain fundamentalist groups who believe that we are not far from the final Apocalypse, when true believers will be transported instantly to heaven, in a state of rapture. The rest of us will be left to experience a miserable fate, as the world inexorably descends into chaos. The word "rapture" has come to express the dangerous fantasy of abandoning the earth, a fantasy that involves the denial that the earth is the matrix within which human destiny has to be fulfilled. This fantasy lies behind several mass suicides of members of small cults in the USA during the

1990s - cults like Heaven's Gate and Solar Temple, where members believed that by committing suicide they released their spirit to travel to heaven, a journey crudely conceived as aided by extra terrestials.

More seriously, and certainly more expensively, there is the powerful technological fantasy of abandoning the earth in a spaceship or dressed in a spacesuit. This is essentially a *dream of disincarnation* symbolised by the new technological shaman, the astronaut (Illustration 1). Plans are now underway to build a space hotel that should be up and running by the year 2020. According to a recent report in *The Times*, it is to be called (would you believe) "Hotel Galactica" and is being designed by Kawasaki. Already six thousand Germans have made reservations (costing £300 each).[9] Whether it happens or not, the project itself is an expression of the desire to desert the real world for the virtual world.

It would seem that the desertion of the real world for the virtual world has already reached epidemic proportions in contemporary society. After sleeping and working, the third largest use of time in the USA and Europe is watching television. It is quite astonishing that this is actually how most people spend most of their leisure time. In a remarkable series of photographs, Jeff Wall has captured the way in which the soul is drawn out of itself to inhabit an inner world that is not its own. Instead of putting us in touch with what is going on in our own soul-life, people are lured into an artificial inner world (Illustration 2).

But this is nothing compared to the possibilities opened up by interactive virtual technology, through which one can have the experience of *literally* entering virtual space. By the 1980s, it was clear that the very term "virtual world" was to signify a new reality. This "reality" came into its own with the development of the "stereoscopic head-mounted display" (that interestingly was first pioneered by NASA) and "data gloves" that provided the means by which one could enter virtual space, and at the same time exit real space (Illustration 3).[10] It is now possible for people in different parts of the world to explore the same virtual reality through a telecommunication link-up. Nowadays there are full body suits which one can wear in order to seal oneself off from the actual space one is in, all the more effectively to enter the virtual space.

The development of virtual technology may be the most obvious example of how strong the fantasy of abandoning the earth is in contemporary society, but it also manifests in countless other ways that are extremely easy to overlook. When you next get into your car, remember that you too are also participating in the dream of disincarnation, for what is a car if not a spaceship on wheels, which not only seals you off from your environment but also enables you to travel at high speed off the ground? The astronaut has, as Robert Romanyshyn argued more than a decade ago in a book called *Technology as Symptom and Dream* (1989), become the unconscious fantasy image, the model of new Technological Humanity.[11] We are all astronauts today. We participate in this fantasy when we listen to our walkman, when we objectify the world through the camera lens, when we communicate with other human beings hundreds or thousands of miles away by telephone, or better still by mobile phone, when we eat frozen food, play the electronic keyboard and surf the net.

But is it just a fantasy? We are perhaps too willing today to ascribe to ourselves, or to the human psyche, forces that in previous cultures were recognised as independent cosmic agencies. Behind the Hymn of the Pearl, there is the tacit acknowledgement that human history is enmeshed within the much vaster cosmic process of the outpouring of the divine into the world and the return of the divine to itself through humanity. What works into human history, as we pass

8

1. The fantasy of abandoning the earth: the astronaut as the new technological shaman.

2. Television: inhabiting an inner world that is not our own. Photo by Jeff Wall.

3. Entering virtual space, exiting real space, equipped with stereoscopic head-mounted display and data gloves.

4. Lucifer, who opposes God's engagement with the
material world. Picture by William Blake.

through the different ages or *yugas*, is not simply human. Insofar as human history is part of the cosmic saga of the self-realization of the divine, we must expect suprahuman agencies to be involved, both in a positive and in a negative or hindering way. Behind the human fantasy of abandoning the earth, then, we may detect a suprahuman being opposed to the outflow of the divine into materiality, and whose will is set against the engagement of God in the material world.

If we were to try to characterise the nature of this suprahuman power further, we could say that its whole wish is to oppose the incarnation of the human spirit in the flesh, and therefore seeks to divert us from fully *being* on earth. Rudolf Steiner identified it with the fallen archangel of Christian tradition, Lucifer (Illustration 4).[12] There is a particularly telling story concerning Lucifer, and how it was that he came to fall. It is told in one of the apocryphal texts of the Old Testament, called *The Books of Adam and Eve*.[13] There it is related that when God first created Adam, he invited all the angels to come and worship his new creation, for into Adam God had instilled a spark of his own divine nature, and he was very pleased that he had been able to create a creature of the earth who was at the same time divine like Himself. And all the angels came and bowed down before Adam. But when Lucifer came, he proudly refused to bow before Adam, saying "What? Am I to bow before this thing of clay! Never!"

In Lucifer's nature, then, there is this hatred of the earth, and opposition to the whole process of the incarnation of the human spirit. Lucifer failed to understand that there could be any meaning in the divine involvement with the material world, and therefore he set his will against it. He is a factor of contemporary life which I believe it is essential to recognise if we are to understand what is really going on today.

The Impulse to Descend

At the other end of the polarity, there is the drive to greater and greater separation from the divine, which if carried to its extreme would result in the ever greater intensification of *Kali Yuga* to the point at which it becomes impossible for a return to take place.

One meets this side of the polarity in the kind of scientific reductionist philosophy where there is flintlike opposition to any view of the world that acknowledges the reality of the spirit. One encounters in early scientific philosophers like Thomas Hobbes or mid 20th century scientists like Francis Crick or Jacques Monod an almost religious fervour in the reductionist project to prove that there is nothing more to life than physical processes. The desire to explain everything without recourse to God has been one of the driving forces behind science since the 17th century. This desire was succinctly expressed by the 18th century mathematician and physicist Laplace when, in conversation with Napoleon, he declared that God was "an unnecessary hypothesis". In the scientific philosophy of Decart, Hobbes and others, which laid the foundations of the philosophical framework of the sciences, only mechanistic explanations were regarded as valid. The physical body came to be seen as a machine.

The view that the human body is a machine has been one of the great rallying causes of scientific reductionism. It is a gauntlet thrown down to challenge our innate sense that human beings are spiritual beings, and in the hands of radicals like Monod it comes across as a mantra that expresses a central truth of the anti-religious philosophy of scientism: "The cell is a machine. The animal is a machine. Man is a machine."[14] In the language of modern reductionist science, human beings are "simply one type of machine, a biological, electrochemical form."[15] This is a view that is no longer regarded as particularly radical. I have a biology textbook written for children, published ten years ago with the title *The Human Machine*. In the introduction, the very first sentence reads, "The human body is a fascinating and remarkable machine. Its design is far more complex than the most advanced computer..."[16] This is a standard modern textbook for children! Turn the pages and you see the different joints in the human skeleton pictured in the clean lines that one would find in any manual of basic engineering: pivot joint, hinge joint, ball and socket joint etc. (Illustration 5)

If the body is a machine, then it can be treated as one would treat a machine. When parts wear out, then you replace them with new parts. "Spare part" surgery covers more and more body parts, from new hip joints and thighbones, to artery replacements and even heart transplants. In the United Kingdom, it was proposed during the summer of 1999 that once a person dies their organs should be made available to anyone else that needs them. At the moment you still have to have a donor card if you are prepared to let your organs be used by someone else. The new proposal - if it became law - would legally establish the principle that the human body is just a conglomeration of parts that are *unensouled*, and that can therefore be removed, swopped or replaced by someone else's equally unensouled body parts.[17] As it is, there is already a massive multi-million dollar trade in "body parts". According to a 1997 report, in the USA alone the market for human organs is worth $6billion per year.[18]

If the human skeleton is nowadays described in terms that would be recognised by any robotics engineer, and different organs are seen virtually as mechanical components that can be replaced as one would an old carburetter or worn out clutch, then when it comes to the brain it is no surprise to find it explained in terms immediately recognisable to a computer technician. The brain is constantly compared to a computer, and the generally accepted view within mainstream science and philosophy is that human consciousness is either a bi-product of complex brain-processes, or is no different from the brain-processes themselves. If the brain is just a "neural computer", then the fantasy of augmenting brain capacity with silicon chip implants comes almost (I hesitate to use the word) naturally.[19]

Back in the 17th century, it was still felt necessary to give a place in the brain to the soul, which Decart thought resided in the pineal gland. Today, the soul, like God in the 17th century, has also become an "unnecessary hypothesis". And this view has insinuated itself into the way people speak and think about their inner life. For example, it is fashionable to talk about "left brain" and "right brain" thinking, as if logical thinking ("left brain") or intuitive, creative thinking ("right brain") are simply brain functions, and the person who is doing the thinking or being creative doesn't exist. It is alarming - the extent to which people are willing to adopt a way of speaking about the soul in terms that actually exclude it.

The Disensouled Body

During the summer of 1999 a teenage girl was forced against her will to have a heart transplant. She said that she did not want someone else's heart and would prefer to die.[20] In any other period in history the very idea of heart transplants would have been considered diabolical, for wasn't the heart where a person's deepest and truest self resided? If we no longer think so today, could this be because we have lost contact with that deepest and truest self? Heart transplants are nowadays conducted on the premise that a person's identity is located in their brain and, as we have seen, it is becoming increasingly acceptable to think of ourselves simply as brains, as if the very concept of soul has become

12

something of an embarrassment to contemporary, computer-literate humans. The case of the girl who was forced to have a heart transplant raises the following question: while in scientific terms the girl's life was saved, her heart was nevertheless cut out of her body and someone else's heart is now in her body. Is she now the same person? Modern transplant surgery raises, for each one of us, the subtle question of where our personal identity begins and ends.

The logical consequence of the view that the body is just a conglomeration of replaceable parts, functioning more or less mechanically, is to replace the body altogether by a machine. It would be more efficient, longer lasting and easier to maintain. This is a suggestion that has been seriously made by various respected scientists throughout the 20th century - from J.D. Bernal (the eminent physicist and historian of science) in the 1920s to Hans Moravec (professor of engineering at MIT) in the 1980s.[21] It is suggested that an operation could be performed to extract the brain and attach it to the latest model of computer, or computerised robot. To Kevin Warwick, Professor of Cybernetics at Reading University, the advantages are so obvious as to be self-evident:

"In this way we would be able to give ourselves a type of immortality, with not only our body being replaced by a new gleaming robot body, but also our brain being replaced by a new, much more powerful, faster, more accurate machine brain."[22]

For the concept is that our own brain pattern (= us) can be transferred across to a much better machine brain whilst retaining all memories and experiences up to that point. On the assumption that the brain alone holds the person's identity and the rest of the body is expendable, how could anyone doubt that our new incarnation in the "post-biological" body of cold metal and electronic circuitry would be anything but an amazing improvement? (Illustration 6) As Arthur C Clarke, who is a staunch advocate of this new machine-human hybrid, points out in his book *Profiles of the Future* (1982), it would also have the great advantage of abolishing the need for sleep, thereby inaugurating a new era in human industriousness.[23] In such ideas we see a hatred not only of the living human organism, but also of the domain which specifically belongs to the life of the soul: the "night world" of sleep, of dreams and of spontaneous feeling.[24] The fantasy of replacing the body with a machine and mechanically augmenting human brain capacity is an expression of a deep impulse to destroy the human soul and bind whatever is left of us to the inorganic or mineral level.

Another expression of this same assault on the integrity of the human being is the more realistic possibility of replacing human organs with organ transplants from genetically modified animal donors, such as pigs. This is very close to being generally practised. In October 1999, ahead of the use of transgenic pig organs, new guidelines were revealed that would require anyone who received one of these organs to sign a declaration that they would not have children.[25] And what if, having signed the declaration, and received the transplant, they nevertheless went ahead and DID have children? Should we not shudder with trepidation at what might emerge into the world?

A safer option than using the organs of transgenic pigs would be to design a new species of creature that would be tailor made to grow organs that would be harvested for human organ transplants.[26] Science has now reached the point at which there now exists the possibility of redesigning animals, plants and also humans. In 1991, over 62,000 transgenic animals were born in British laboratories alone.[27] These included the transgenic mouse ("oncomouse") specially designed so that it is prone to develop cancer, a new "low fat" pig with lower than normal fat (this was achieved by introducing human and mouse genes into the pig's DNA), a new breed of featherless chicken, salmon that grow twice as

14

fast as normal, and so on.[28] Work is still proceeding to design cows that produce human breast milk. In the plant world, there is the infamous genetically modified soya that is resistant to herbicide, the tomatoes with fish genes added to them, rice with added vitamins, and now work is progressing on the redesigning of the oak tree so that it grows faster and straighter.[29] These are just a handful of examples, and we are only at the beginning of a vast and awesome project.

Storming God's Realm

The introduction of genetic material that properly belongs to one species (like the human being) into a quite different species (like the pig) that would never naturally reproduce with the first species, constitutes a violation of the spiritual or archetypal basis of the species interfered with - its intrinsic wholeness and integrity. Through the influence of Darwinist thinking, the idea of the natural world being grounded in spiritual archetypes has long since been discarded, of course, but with consequences that Darwin himself probably did not foresee. The consequences of Darwin's purely materialistic vision of the evolution of species through the mechanism of natural selection is that, once it becomes technologically possible for human beings to act like God and redesign nature, there is no metaphysical or ethical restraint that might prevent the natural and spiritual boundaries of species from being violated. It was this perception that lay behind Prince Charles' comment that "genetic modification takes mankind into realms that belong to God and to God alone."[30] For such uses of genetic engineering biotechnology constitute an invasion of these realms by a purely secular and utilitarian consciousness, driven by big business and with the powerful motivation of making big money.[31] No doubt within the medical world, there are genuinely altruistic motives guiding research, but the metaphysical and ethical question as to our treatment of

15

species that are being manipulated, distorted and sacrificed for human wellbeing casts a deep shadow over such altruism.

The idea that animals and plants might have intrinsic rights, that they might have an intrinsic value, must of necessity be excluded from research programmes geared towards their "improvement" from our human point of view. Once one begins to think in terms of how other species can be "improved" for human benefit, a certain corruption of the human soul sets in. An example of the way this type of thinking, exalted by its own wizardry, can take hold of people is the suggestion made by Patrick Dixon, in his book *The Genetic Revolution* (1995):

> "There is no logical or practical reason why we cannot give human genes to chimpanzees with the aim of giving them a spoken language... Perhaps we could use them as intelligent subhuman clones for difficult and dangerous tasks, instead of incredibly expensive and limited robots."[32]

Here we see how seductively this purely instrumental way of thinking engages in an all out assault on the spiritual integrity of the organic world. Such an assault could only take place within a mentality that is not just Godless but is in a real sense diabolical, a mentality that has corroded the human soul with its diabolical cleverness.[33]

Unfortunately, Patrick Dixon's dream of subhuman chimpanzee clones is not unrealisable. It is likely that genetic research will eventually produce new species that fall half-way between human and animal. We are already well on the way to Frankenstein's monster. It has always struck me as ironic that in the popular imagination the name Frankenstein has become synonymous with the monster, when in fact Frankenstein was the human creator of the monster. Should we not take this as a warning about our own forthcoming fate? The more monstrous new forms we create, the more

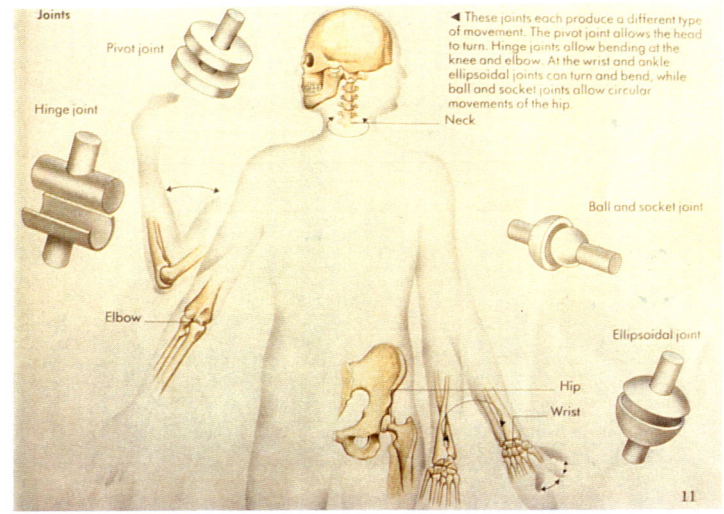

Joints

Pivot joint

Hinge joint

◄ These joints each produce a different type of movement. The pivot joint allows the head to turn. Hinge joints allow bending at the knee and elbow. At the wrist and ankle ellipsoidal joints can turn and bend, while ball and socket joints allow circular movements of the hip.

Neck

Ball and socket joint

Elbow

Ellipsoidal joint

Hip

Wrist

11

5. *"The human body is a fascinating and remarkable machine."*
Illustration from a biology textbook for children.

WABOT-2

6. *How could a body of cold metal and electronic circuitry*
be anything but an amazing improvement?
A Japanese robot plays the piano.

7. Frankenstein's monster: the more monstrous new forms we create, the more monstrous we ourselves will become.

8. The archangel Michael struggling as much to free himself from the Satanic power as to bind it. Picture by William Blake.

monstrous will our own human nature have surely become. (Illustration 7)

Behind this drive to desacralise and to desecrate both nature and the human being there is something more than simply human involved. For there is something more than simply human that is at stake. In terms of the Hymn of the Pearl, there is a pearl at stake, the symbol of the divine within the world of nature. We need to recognise that the brilliant but unscrupulous intelligence we utilise to bring about the desacralisation of nature, and to convince ourselves that the human soul and spirit are figments of an outmoded worldview, should be thought of as an independent force within the cosmos and within history. For it is the primary factor that carries the cosmic impulse toward separation from the divine. Humanity has had to submit to this impulse in order to become fully independent of the "parental" world of its spiritual origins. Only then could there develop the possibility of a truly free return. But the impulse toward separation does not itself harbour any kindly undertow that would draw us back to the divine world of the Mother/Father God. On the contrary, it is only to the extent that we succeed in overcoming it, as the prince succeeded in overcoming the serpent, that the return becomes possible.

If we were to personify this force, we would have to say that it seeks to drive out any residual awareness that God is present in nature, or that the human being is in any way capable of embodying divinity. Rather, it would lead us further and further from the spiritual world into a subearthly, subhuman realm. William Blake characterised it in two ways: in so far as it operates within human consciousness, it appears as the figure of Urizen - human intelligence bound within the "single vision" of purely secular and rational thinking. But in its more cosmic aspect, Blake saw it as the being that in Christianity is referred to as Satan, who is distinguished from the light-loving Lucifer by his traditionally

17

heavy and serpentine form.[34] In Blake's famous illustration of "Michael binding Satan" (Illustration 8), Michael is portrayed as the representative of humanity, struggling as much to free himself from the power of the serpent as to bind it. Indeed, there is an ambivalence about who is binding who, and the outcome is by no means certain.

An Uncertain Outcome

It is the opinion of many commentators that we are now in the very depths of *Kali Yuga*. In terms of the Hymn of the Pearl, we should still be waiting for the eagle to arrive and wake us from our slumbers. I don't think this view is right. According to Steiner, the *Kali Yuga* ended before the 20th century even began, in 1899. If you ask how it could be that our century has seen more people killed in wars than ever before, probably more people killed in famines and more natural environments ruined than ever before, the first completely atheist regimes in the old Soviet Union and China, which also happened to be the most brutal tyrannies that have ever existed, we might take encouragement from the words of C.G. Jung, who said (I paraphrase), "there is always an outburst of the destructive powers when a hero is born".[35] There is something that is struggling to come to birth within human consciousness today that would truly inaugurate a new spiritual era. But at such moments of delicate new beginnings, we must expect the activity of the Opposition to intensify.

Even if *Kali Yuga* has "officially" ended, this does not mean the new age of light will automatically begin. There is actually the danger that, instead of the return, the momentum downwards will carry us even further away from the spiritual world. We are living at a crucial period in the history of humanity, a period that could be described as humanity's

18

biggest test.[36] Do we get ever more sucked into the materialist worldview, utilitarian ethic and lifestyle, or do we forge a way forward and upward toward fully conscious reunion with the divine? In order to do this, both the "Luciferic" temptation to return without the pearl, and the "Satanic" temptation to live by the sterile light of an intellect divorced from spiritual insight must be overcome. The impulse toward separation and independence needs to be married with the buried yearning to return, just as the impulse to see our true destiny as lying beyond the world needs to be tempered by the recognition that there is a pearl to be won here on Earth.

In terms of the Hymn of the Pearl, we are no longer in the position of waiting for the eagle to appear, to rouse us and guide us toward our spiritual home. The fact is, at least three eagles have already been sent down into the Western world during the 20th century. We have had Jung and the foundation of depth psychology, we have had Steiner's renewal of the Western esoteric tradition and we have had the influx of Buddhist philosophy and meditation practice into the Western world. These are three major spiritual gifts that the 20th century has received, amongst others. The onus is entirely on us, on each one of us, to negotiate a course that embraces what is positive within the two polar tendencies intrinsic to the cosmic drama of descent and return, and as individuals to go forth, find and return with the pearl.

On the urgency of our earnestly engaging in this quest, no one has written more passionately and eloquently than the Sufi mystic and poet, Rumi:

> "There is one thing in this world which you must never forget to do. If you forget everything else and not this, there's nothing to worry about, but if you remember everything else and forget this, then you will have done nothing with your life.

> It's as if a king has sent you to some country to do a

*task, and you perform a hundred other services, but
not the one he sent you to do. And not doing it
is like using a priceless Indian sword to slice rotten
meat, or like cooking turnips in a golden bowl, or like
thrusting the finest tempered knife into a wall so
you can hang things from it.*

*You may say, "But look, I'm using the knife. It is not
lying idle." Do you hear how ludicrous that sounds?
Any old iron nail could be used for the same
purpose. You may say, "But I spend my energies on
lofty pursuits. I study Law and Philosophy and
Astronomy and Medicine and all the rest". But
consider why you do those things. They are all
branches of yourself.*

*Remember the deep root of your being, the inner
presence of God. Give your life to the one who
already owns your breath and your every moment.
If you don't, you will be exactly like the person who
hammers a precious knife into the kitchen wall and
uses it for a peg on which to hang some pot. You
will be wasting the keenness of your life and
foolishly ignoring your true dignity and your
purpose."37*

Notes and References

1 For sources of this tradition, see R.C. Zaehner, *Hinduism* (New York, Oxford University Press, 1966) p.62. A more detailed discussion (including the Buddhist versions of the teaching) is to be found in Mircea Eliade, *The Myth of the Eternal Return* (Princeton, Princeton University Press, 1954) p.112ff. The tradition is taken up into Western esotericism at the end of the 19th century through the Theosophical movement (for example in the writings of A.P. Sinnett, W.Q. Judge, Annie Besant and others), and then at the beginning of the 20th century in Rudolf Steiner's Anthroposophy. For the latter, see Stewart Easton, *Man and the World in the Light of Anthroposophy* (New York, Anthroposophic Press, 1975) Ch.2. It is also referred to with critical reference to the present times from the standpoint of traditional metaphysics in René Guénon, *The Reign of Quantity and the Signs of the Times* (London, Luzac and Co, 1953).

2 The specific dates of the beginning and ending of *Kali Yuga* are not generally agreed upon. I have followed Rudolf Steiner's dating, viz 3100BC-AD1899. See Stewart Easton, *Man and the World in the Light of Anthroposophy* p.34.

3 René Guénon, *The Reign of Quantity* Ch.17.

4 Hesiod, *Works and Days* 105ff.

5 Mircea Eliade, *The Myth of the Eternal Return* p.124f.

6 See Jeremy Naydler, *Temple of the Cosmos* (Rochester, VT, Inner Traditions International, 1996)

Chapter 5.

7   "The Hymn of the Pearl", translated by Willis Barnstone
     in Willis Barnstone (ed), *The Other Bible* (San
     Francisco, Harper and Row, 1984). I have simplified
     the story in the account that follows. For a commentary
     on the Hymn of the Pearl, see Hans Jonas, *The
     Gnostic Religion* (Boston, Beacon Press, 1963).

8   Mircea Eliade has frequently commented on this. See
     for example his *Myths, Dreams and Mysteries* Ch.3
     on "the nostalgia for paradise", and *The Myth of the
     Eternal Return* Ch.4 on "the terror of history".

9   *The Times* October 2nd, 1999, p.15.

10   Frank Popper, *Art of the Electronic Age* (London,
     Thames and Hudson, 1993), p.112. See also Ziauddin
     Sardar and Jerome R. Ravetz (eds), *Cyberfutures*
     (London, Pluto Press, 1996).

11   Robert D. Romanyshyn, *Technology as Symptom and
     Dream* (London, Routledge, 1989). See also Noel
     Cobb's brilliant reveiw "Technology's Dream of
     Abandoning Earth" in *Temenos* 11 (London, 1990)
     p.247ff.

12   Rudolf Steiner, *The Influences of Lucifer and Ahriman*
     (London, Rudolf Steiner Publishing Co, 1954).

13   "Vita Adae et Evae" in R.H. Charles, *The Apocrypha
     and Pseudepigraphia of the Old Testament in English*
     Vol 2 (Oxford, Oxford University Press, 1913) p.137.

14   Quoted in Kevin Warwick, *The March of the Machines*

(London, Century, 1997) p.142.

15 Kevin Warwick, Ibid. p.143.

16 Brenda Walpole, *The Human Machine* (Hove, Wayland, 1990), p.5.

17 Despite the Government's rejection of the proposal on July 16, 1999, the pressure to install a system of "presumed consent" to replace the current "opt in" system of donor cards is bound to intensify as the demand for organs increases. See *The Independent* 17 July, 1999, p.5.

18 *The Guardian* (Society) March 5, 1997, p.4.

19 The vision of the brain as a "neural computer" is set forth in Steven Pinker, *How the Mind Works* (New York, Norton, 1998). For Kevin Warwick, Professor of Cybernetics at Reading University, the difference between machine brains and human brains is a purely quantitative difference of scale: "The performance of machine brains is undoubtedly getting closer and closer to that of human brains... The one problem which remains is scaling up. We now have artificial neural networks which operate with 50 or 1000 neurons, but to compete with human brains these networks must contain billions of neurons..." *The March of the Machines* p.144.

20 *The Times* 16 July, 1999.

21 J.D. Bernal, *The World, the Flesh and the Devil* (1929); Hans Moravec, *Mind Children: The Future of Robot and Human Intelligence* (Cambridge Mass, Harvard University Press, 1988). See also William Irwin

Thompson's discussion in *The American Replacement of Nature* (New York, Bantam Doubleday Dell, 1991) p.122ff.

22   Kevin Warwick, *The March of the Machines*, p146.

23   Arthur C Clarke, *Profiles of the Future* (London, Victor Gollancz, 1982) p.221f.

24   For a discussion of the enmity of reductionist science and "the dark mind" of the unconscious psyche, see Theodore Roszak, *Where the Wasteland Ends* (London, Faber and Faber, 1972) Ch.3.

25   The guidelines were in a report drawn up by the Government sponsored infection surveillance steering group of the U.K. xeno-transplantation interim regulatory authority (UKXIRA) and appear on the front page of *The Daily Telegraph* October 25, 1999.

26   Patrick Dixon, *The Genetic Revolution* (Eastbourne, Kingsway Publications, 1995), Ch.4.

27   *New Scientist* (November 11, 1992) p.13.

28   See Patrick Dixon, *The Genetic Revolution* p.89ff. The many problematic, and often fatal, side-effects to which genetically modified animals are susceptible have been repeatedly pointed out by Mae-Wan Ho. See, for example, Mae-Wan Ho, Hartmut Meyer and Joe Cummins, "The Biotechnology Bubble" in *The Ecologist* (May/June 1998), p.149 and Mae-Wan Ho, *Genetic Engineering: Dream or Nightmare?* (Wellow, Gateways Books, 1998) Chapter 9 and Chapter 11.

29   Patrick Dixon, *The Genetic Revolution* p.85ff. On the genetic modification of oaks and other trees, see Matthew Wenban-Smith, "Something Nasty in the Woodshed?" in *Living Earth (Magazine of the Soil Association)* April/June 1999, p.10f.

30   HRH The Prince of Wales, "Seeds of Disaster" *The Ecologist* (Sept/Oct 1998), p.252.

31   For the involvement of big business in genetic engineering biotechnology, Mae-Wan Ho, *Genetic Engineering: Dream or Nightmare?* Chapter 1.

32   Patrick Dixon, Op cit p.76.

33   For an incisive discussion on the corrosive power of reason divorced from a guiding spiritual principle, see Seyyed Hossein Nasr, *Man and Nature* (London, Mandala, 1976), Ch.1, and particularly p.20.

34   Rudolf Steiner identified this being with the the ancient Persian god of darkness and sterility, Ahriman, the opponent of Ormuzd (or Ahura Mazda) the god of light. Rudolf Steiner, *The Influences of Lucifer and Ahriman* (London, Rudolf Steiner Publishing Co., 1954).

35   See Marie-Louise von Franz, *Alchemy* (Toronto, Inner City Books, 1980) p.225.

36   Peter Tradowsky, *Christ and Antichrist* (London, Temple Lodge, 1998) p.72.

37   "The One Thing You Must Do" in Jelaluddin Rumi, *Say I Am You* translated by Coleman Barks (Maypop Press, 1994) p.21 (slightly adapted).

Illustration Sources

1   The fantasy of abandoning the earth. From Gregory
    Vogt, *Spaceships* (London, Franklin Watts, 1990) p.21.

2   Inhabiting an inner world that is not our own. "Movie
    Audience" by Jeff Wall (1979) reproduced from Jürgen
    Tesch, *Icons of Art: the 20th Century* (New York,
    Prestel , 1981), p.204.

3   Entering virtual space, exiting real space. From Frank
    Popper, *Art of the Electronic Age* (London, Thames and
    Hudson, 1993) p.112.

4   Lucifer, who refuses to accept God's involvement with
    matter. Picture by William Blake, reproduced in
    Peter Lambourn Wilson, *Angels* (London, Thames and
    Hudson, 1980) Plate 5.

5   "The human body is a fascinating and remarkable
    machine". Reproduced from Brenda Walpole, *The
    Human Machine* (Hove, Wayland, 1990) p.11.

6   How could a body of cold metal and electronic circuitry
    be anything but an amazing improvement? Japanese
    robot playing the piano, reproduced from Rhys Lewis,
    The Computer Age (Hove, Wayland,1991) p.38.

7   Frankenstein's monster: a warning about our own
    forthcoming fate? Reproduced from David Barrett,
    Destiny and Your Dreams (Enderby, Acropolis Books,
    1992) p.25.

8   Archangel Michael struggling as much to free himself
    from the Satanic power as to bind it. Picture by William
    Blake (c.1805), reproduced in Kathleen Raine, *William
    Blake* (London, Thames and Hudson, 1970) pl.91.